2020

To Jay on your 50th
birthday

"Try not to become
a man of success,
but rather, try to

become a man
of value.
    — Albert Einstein

Taking life one day at
a time — enjoying the
simple things of life
the most — I know you
do this in your life!
May God continue to bless you
abundantly —

Love,
Cindy

TO

FROM

DATE

COURAGE

Copyright © 1997 by Garborg's Heart 'n Home, Inc.

Published by Garborg's Heart 'n Home, Inc.
P. O. Box 20132, Bloomington, MN 55420

Art Copyright © Scott Kennedy

For information regarding Scott Kennedy's paintings contact
Greenwich Workshop, Inc. at 1-800-243-4246.

Design by Mick Thurber

ISBN 1-881830-41-1

COURAGE

COURAGE TO
OVERCOME

No matter
how difficult the
challenge, when we
spread our wings
of faith and allow
the winds of God's
Spirit to lift us, no
obstacle is too great
to overcome.

ROY LESSIN

The eagle flies in storms while other birds seek shelter and other animals run and hide. With an adjustment of his wings, the eagle can fly almost motionless even in the face of great winds. The eagle uses the strong winds of the storm to lift him higher and higher until he rises above the clouds. The eagle has no power to stop a storm, but he knows how to overcome without fear.

KENNETH PRICE

To overcome a difficulty in your life:
believe in the character of God...
He is good;
believe in the power of God...
He will bring you through;
believe in the love of God...He cares for
you deeply and He will not abandon you.

ROY LESSIN

It's the set of the soul that decides the goal, and not the storms of life.

ELLA WHEELER WILCOX

Keep trying. It's only from
the valley that the mountain
seems so high.

Accept whatever comes
and...meet it with courage
and with the best that
you have to give.

ELEANOR ROOSEVELT

When you get into a tight
place and everything goes
against you, till it seems as
though you could not hang on
a minute longer, never give
up then, for that is just the
place and time that the
tide will turn.

HARRIET BEECHER STOWE

We are lifted above our circumstances when we look into the face of Jesus.

GIGI GRAHAM
TCHIVIDJIAN

Down through the centuries in times of trouble and trial God has brought courage to the hearts of those who love Him. The Bible is filled with assurances of God's help and comfort in every kind of trouble which might cause fears to arise in the human heart. You can look ahead with promise, hope, and joy.

BILLY GRAHAM

God wants to give you the strength and skill to climb your troublesome mountain and stand at last triumphant at the top!

GLORIA GAITHER

The world is full of suffering. It is also full of the overcoming of it. We could never learn to be brave and patient if there were only joy in the world.... Character cannot be developed in ease and quiet. Only through the experience of trial and suffering can the soul be strengthened, vision cleared, ambition inspired, and success achieved.

HELEN KELLER

Do not pray for easy lives.
Pray to be stronger. Do not pray for
tasks equal to your powers. Pray for
powers equal to your tasks.

PHILLIPS BROOKS

You can come out the furnace of
trouble two ways: if you let it consume
you, you come out a cinder; but there is
a kind of metal which refuses to be
consumed, and comes out a star.

JEAN CHURCH

Courage is when you do what you have to do though people don't think you can. Courage is when you think you can't do something, but you do it. Courage is when you are down and out and all the odds are against you, and you come out on top; it's when you stare your worst fear or toughest obstacle in the face and beat it. Courage is when you take on the impossible or fight an unwinnable fight. That's what courage is.

ADAM MCCORD, TEENAGER PARALYZED
IN AN AUTOMOBILE ACCIDENT

One of God's most
majestic creatures challenges
us to look at our difficulties
from a broader perspective—
the soaring eagle never
worries how he will cross
a raging river.

ROY LESSIN

COURAGE TO
LIVE WHAT
YOU BELIEVE

A man who is willing
to follow God may not
always do what is popular
or convenient, but he will
do what is right and good.
Then he will have no regrets
if others choose to follow
his example.

ROY LESSIN

Follow my example,
as I follow the example
of Christ.

1 CORINTHIANS 11:1

Courage is the first of
human qualities, because
it is the quality which
guarantees all others.

WINSTON S. CHURCHILL

Give to us clear vision that we may know where to stand and what to stand for. Let us not be content to wait and see what will happen, but give us the determination to make the right things happen.

PETER MARSHALL

I *am not bound to win, but I am bound to be true: I am not bound to succeed, but I am bound to live up to what light I have.*

ABRAHAM LINCOLN

Try not to become a man of success,
but rather, try to become
a man of value.

ALBERT EINSTEIN

May God give us a pure heart
    so we may see Him;
A humble heart so we may hear Him;
A loving heart so we may serve Him;
A faithful heart so we may live Him.

DAG HAMMARSKJOLD

Integrity in all
things precedes
all else. The open
demonstration of
integrity is essential.

MAX DEPREE

The visibility of courage is very much heightened during the times of crisis and turmoil. But there are other less visible forms of courage—courage to do your best each day when there are no mountaintop experiences to keep you going; courage to say no when "everyone is doing it"; courage to permit compromise; courage to stand your ground on things that should not be compromised.

LES SONNABEND

The storms of life can be used for good in our lives if we let them drive our spirits higher and closer to God.

ROY LESSIN

Make the most of every opportunity you have for doing good. Don't act thoughtlessly, but try to find out and do whatever the Lord wants you to do.

EPHESIANS 5:16,17 TLB

Without belittling the courage with which men have died, we should not forget those acts of courage with which men...have lived. The courage of life is often a less dramatic spectacle than the courage of a final moment; but it is no less a magnificent mixture of triumph and tragedy. A man does what he must—in spite of personal consequences, in spite of obstacles and dangers and pressures—and that is the basis of all human morality....

*In whatever arena of life
one may meet the challenge
of courage, whatever may
be the sacrifices he faces if he
follows his conscience—the loss
of his friends, his fortune, his
contentment, even the esteem
of his fellow men—each man
must decide for himself the
course he will follow.*

JOHN F. KENNEDY

COURAGE
TO ENDURE

Nothing worthwhile ever
happens quickly and easily.
You achieve only as you are
determined to achieve...and
as you keep at it until
you have achieved.

ROBERT H. LAUER

Nothing is easier than saying words. Nothing is harder than living them, day after day. What you promise today must be renewed and redecided tomorrow and each day that stretches out before you.

ARTHUR GORDON

The man who lives for God is not in a sprint, but in a long distance race. He does not look for instant gratification, but has his eye on eternal goals.

ROY LESSIN

Let us throw
off everything
that hinders...and
let us run with
perseverance the
race marked
out for us.

HEBREWS 12:1

Do not lose courage in considering
your own imperfections, but instantly
set about remedying them—every day
begin the task anew...

We will steer safely through every storm, as long as our heart is right, our intention fervent, our courage steadfast, and our trust fixed on God.

FRANCIS DE SALES

It is only by thinking about great and good things that we come to love them, and it is only by loving them that we come to long for them, and it is only by longing for them that we are impelled to seek after them; and it is only by seeking after them that they become ours.

HENRY VAN DYKE

No created being can ever know how much and how sweetly and tenderly God loves them. It is only with the help of His grace that we are able to persevere... with endless wonder at His high, surpassing, immeasurable love.

JULIAN OF NORWICH

Keep alert, stand firm in
your faith, be courageous,
be strong.

1 CORINTHIANS 16:13 NRSV

Do not fear tomorrow,
God is already there.

Lives of great men all remind us,
we can make our life sublime,
and departing, leave behind us
footprints on the sands of time....
Let us then be up and doing,
with a heart for any fate;
still achieving, still pursuing.
Learn to labor and to wait.

HENRY WADSWORTH LONGFELLOW

BEHIND THE SCENE

"I paint because I feel that's what God wants me to do with the talent He's given me. It's not only a pleasure, but also an act of reverence to paint what I see around me," says Scott Kennedy. A Colorado native and well-known wilderness artist, Kennedy sets the scene for the painting used on this product.

"Wings on the Wind"

We live by some lakes that are home to and visited by a multitude of birds. Blue herons, American pelicans, ducks, and Canadian geese to name a few. Yet none are more exciting to see than occasional bald eagles. They are usually perched silently in the cottonwoods at the shore's edge. Yet to the lucky spectator the thrill of witnessing them take flight is an experience that never grows old.

"Wings on the Wind" is a painting in which I have tried to capture this drama of a bald eagle in flight. Watching an eagle spread its wings and soar is captivating. I don't know why, but perhaps in part it is because our souls long to experience their effortless freedom. Eagles are recognized worldwide as a symbol of freedom and power. One of my favorite quotes from the Bible is God's promise to Israel that "they will soar on wings like an eagle"—an exciting prospect to consider if you have recently witnessed the drama of this amazing bird's flight.